NATIONAL UNIVERSITY
LIBRARY   SAN DIEGO

Super Sub

A Must-Have Handbook for Substitute Teachers

By Cary Seeman and Shannon Hofstrand

Good Year Books

Parsippany, New Jersey

Dedication

To Eryn Sydney Pate,
Cary's granddaughter
and Shannon's daughter.

Good Year Books are available for most basic curriculum subjects plus many enrichment areas. For more Good Year Books, contact your local bookseller or educational dealer. For a complete catalog with information about other Good Year Books, please write:

Good Year Books
An imprint of Pearson Learning
299 Jefferson Road
Parsippany, New Jersey 07054-0480
1-800-321-3106
www.pearsonlearning.com

Design and Illustration: Amy O'Brien Krupp

ISBN 0-673-36380-5

5 6 7 8 9 - ML - 06 05 04 03 02 01 00

Table of Contents

Preface

★ "Be Prepared" is more than just the Boy Scout motto. Substitute teachers quickly learn that preparedness can mean the difference between a successful day and a harried, out-of-control one. Even when called at the last minute, or left with meager daily plans, substitutes *can* be ready to go. Our book guarantees it!

We have included lesson plans to fit every curriculum area, as well as behavior control ideas to help keep the class on track. Each lesson requires minimum preparation time and readily available supplies.

This book is meant to be a useful teaching tool. Go ahead and write in it. Keep notes on what works for you. Modify the plans to suit your needs and personality. Use the Substitute Travelogue to keep track of the classrooms you've worked in and the lessons you've used. By keeping a written record, you won't have to remember whether you've already used a lesson with a particular class.

Have fun with the lessons. You are prepared to teach!

PART I

The Preliminary Tools

The Sub Kit

Dos and Don'ts

Substitute Travelogue

The Dos and Don'ts of Substituting

1. Do speak in a whisper for attention. Students have to be quiet to hear what you're saying.

Don't raise your voice. Kids are used to being yelled at, and it doesn't faze them at all.

2. Do correct papers for the assignments you issued. The teacher doesn't want to return to a stack of unmarked papers.

Don't send papers home without letting the classroom teacher see them first.

3. Do arrange an audible signal (such as a whistle) before you take students out on the playground. You may have to recall them in a hurry.

Don't release students outside without reinforcing rules (time-out spot, boundaries, etc.).

4. Do familiarize yourself with school and classroom rules before class convenes.

Don't expect the students to interpret the classroom and school rules accurately for you. ("We're allowed to sit on the floor for math"; "Tuesday is extra recess day"; "Ms. Smith said we have until tomorrow to study for the quiz.")

5. Do be sure to obtain accurate directions to the school before starting out in the morning.

Don't be the last to arrive and the first to leave the building.

6. Do notify the teacher next door if an emergency occurs.

Don't leave students unattended, even if personal needs arise.

7. Do attempt to sit with staff in the faculty room during breaks and lunch.

Don't isolate yourself in the classroom. You may make some good contacts by getting to know other staff members.

8. Do walk your students to specialists' classes (music, PE, etc.).

Don't allow students to move through the school unattended.

9. Do encourage students with positive comments.

Don't point out problem areas in a student's work until voicing at least one compliment.

10. Do develop motivating rewards (five extra minutes of recess, a quick game, etc.) to elicit desired behavior.

Don't dwell on negative behaviors.

The Sub Kit

W e suggest that you put together a special kit and carry it with you to the classroom. Armed with your Sub Kit, you'll not need to dig through the teacher's desk to find supplies.

Assemble in a canvas bag:

1. This book

2. A stapler and extra staples

3. Adhesive tape and dispenser

4. A box of paper clips (large and small)

5. Scissors

6. Two black permanent markers and a set of colored markers

7. Whistle (important behavior control device on the playground)

8. Extra pencils or pens

9. Masking tape

10. White typing paper (a few sheets)

11. Read-aloud books (where each chapter is a new episode) such as *Pippi Longstocking* or *Sideways Stories from Wayside School*

12. A thesaurus

13. A paperback dictionary

14. Two clean transparencies

15. A dry erase marker

16. Tissues

17. Construction paper

18. Graph paper

19. Ruler

20. Glue

Optional:

- Colored index cards (*see Grouping Ideas, page 10*)

- Mood music tape (Most classrooms have tape players.)

- Basic first-aid kit

- Math flashcards (for quick activity)

- Ordinary playing cards (*see Grouping Ideas, page 9*)

- Sewing kit

- Coffee cup

- "Mystery Box" (*see activity p. 13*)

- Small prizes (stickers or a stamper to stamp hands)

Substitute Travelogue

It is very important to keep information about each classroom in which you substitute. Copy and use the form on the following page to record facts about each school and individual classroom you visit.

Keeping pertinent facts about each teaching experience, and special notes about students with whom you come into contact, can really help you plan for a day in the classroom. Be sure to note activities and classroom management strategies that work and include any extension ideas that you may devise.

Getting to know the head secretaries and daytime custodians by name can be invaluable. Secretaries can get supplies and forms for you and may even have information about upcoming teaching positions. (In some schools, the head secretary even calls the district office to request substitutes.) Maintaining a positive relationship with the school secretaries will help keep your name fresh in their minds. Custodians can help you find supplies and may even assist with some class projects.

Substitute Travelogue

School _____

Principal _____

Head secretary _____

Custodian _____

Opening time _____

Dismissal time _____

Directions to school _____

_____

_____

_____

Teacher's Name _____

Room number _____ Date(s) _____

Grade level _____

Subject area (if applicable) _____

Helpful students _____

Activities tried _____

_____

_____

_____

Additional notes _____

_____

_____

_____

SCHOOL

Substitute Travelogue

Today's Schedule Highlights

Use the form that follows to highlight important events that occur in a day. Covering the form with a clean transparency eliminates the need to copy the form, and since highlights change from class to class, the transparency can simply be wiped clean.

7

Today's Schedule Highlights

Recess times: AM _____

PM _____

Lunch time: _____

Where do kids eat? _____

Specialist(s) time(s):

Library: _____

Music: _____

Physical Education: _____

Computer: _____

Band: _____

Other: _____

Other schedule changes (assemblies, speakers, parent volunteers, fire drills, etc.)

_____

_____

_____

_____

Pairing and Grouping of Students

Have students work in pairs or small groups whenever possible. This allows everyone to experience some degree of success, whether they have special needs or tend to be the top scholars in the class. It also gives students the opportunity to share ideas with their peers, which they will be increasingly expected to do as their educations advance. Finally, it offers students who have difficulty sitting and listening the opportunity to move and talk. Here are some ideas for forming pairs or small groups:

- Shuffle and deal out regular playing cards. Use two, three, or four of one number or picture card depending on the size of the groups you want. Then put all the sevens together, the aces together, the threes together, and so on.

- Pass out squares of colored construction paper to each student. Have all those who receive yellow slips work together, as do all the blues, all the greens, and so on.

- When choosing teams, have captains select group members in the usual way. Then, when the teams are complete, the captains draw numbers to decide which team is theirs. In this way, the captains

aren't necessarily choosing the team they will head.

- Make two equal lines of students. (This gives droopy or wiggly students the opportunity to move.) Then, simply pair the first student of each line, the second of each line, and so on. To line up students easily and quietly, tell them to stand from shortest to tallest. Then, divide the line in two.

- Use the line numbers inside the grade book to pair students. Simply divide the number of students in the class by two, and then pair the stu-

SCHOOL: _____

TEACHER: _____ GRADE: _____

Student's full name: _____

One talent you possess: _____

Favorite subject or hero or career goal:

_____

_____

_____

dent on line one with the student on the line number that is one over halfway through the total. (If there are thirty students in class, pair the student on line one with the student on line sixteen, the student on line two with the student on line seventeen, etc.)

- Begin compiling a set of colored index cards. Use a different color for each school in which you substitute.

Each time you work in a new classroom, have each student fill out an index card with the information above.

(Note: Change the categories as you see fit to gather information that best helps you get to know the students.)

Collect the completed cards. They can be used in a variety of ways: shuffle the cards and use them to put students in groups; use them to get volunteers to read aloud or answer questions. Rubber band class sets together and place in your Sub Kit. You may also make notes about individual students on the cards—if they are helpful, talkative, hardworking, etc. (Be sure to update cards, adding new students and eliminating the cards of those who have moved.)

Practical Ideas for Classroom Management and Motivation

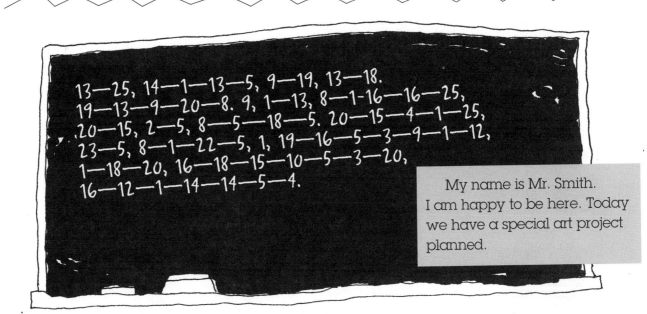

13—25, 14—1—13—5, 9—19, 13—18.
19—13—9—20—8. 9, 1—13, 8—1-16—16—25,
20—15, 2—5, 8—5—18—5. 20—15—4—1—25,
23—5, 8—1—22—5, 1, 19—16—5—3—9—1—12,
1—18—20, 16—18—15—10—5—3—20,
16—12—1—14—14—5—4.

My name is Mr. Smith. I am happy to be here. Today we have a special art project planned.

Behavior and motivation are important parts of the classroom climate. Here are some suggestions to help you make the classroom experience a pleasant one for you and the students.

- To begin the day and get the students settled quickly, write a message in code on the board or overhead projector before the students arrive. Using the code 1=A, 2=B, 3=C, and so on, let the class decipher your opening welcome.

- Compose a simple letter introducing yourself to the class. Tell about your family, pets, hobbies, and so on.

Then, ask each class member to write back, telling a bit about himself or herself. (This activity will show the students that you are interested in them individually.) Read the responses to yourself at recess or lunch, and then share some observations with the class.

- Use a variety of ways to get students to line up for music, recess, or other activities outside the classroom. For instance, use birthday months, starting with those born in January. Older students can then be more specific and line up by the day of the month as well. Have them assemble without talking to add another dimension of communication.

- Let partners work together on a math sheet, language paper, or other assignment having one student do the even numbers, and the partner do the odd numbers. Then partners can swap papers and check each other's work. (Although the students are required to do half the sheet, they actually work the whole sheet when checking, and you eliminate complaints about having to do it all.)

- Announce early in the day that if students have a good morning, they can change seats for the last hour of the day.

- When trying to quiet the class for a certain activity, explain the directions and then have the students close their eyes and imagine what the project will be like. Ask them to describe what they see, how they feel, and what the outcome will be.

(This is a quiet way to involve students and prepare them to work on the assignment.)

- Upon arriving at school, find out where students go in case of a fire drill, to eliminate any confusion.

- Set up a "time-out" area in a quiet corner of the classroom. When two students disagree, send them there. The two must face each other, and each tells his or her side of the story, without interruptions. Neither student may leave the corner until the matter has been settled. (Role-play this system in front of the class before an incident occurs so that everyone will understand the expectations.)

- Bring a sealed "mystery box" to class. Possible contents include foods, flowers, herbs, spices. Let the students hold it, shake it, smell it, and so on. Ask them to write down what they think it is in the box. At the end of the day, reveal the contents and see if anyone correctly guessed it. To make it easier, you might give clues every hour to help solve the mystery. As an alternative to traditional prizes, winners can be dismissed from class first, or allowed to stand at the front of the line.

- Place a clean transparency over the class seating chart. Then, place a plus on each student's name when the student is helpful, hardworking, or positive toward other students. Use a minus to subtract points from unruly students. Three pluses can result in a privilege or prize (stickers, stamps on hands, etc.). Three minuses can be the catalyst for a penalty (time-out, detention, note to teacher, office visit, etc.). Alternately, use the same method with groups of students (tables, rows, etc.) with privileges earned for all students in the winning group at the end of the day.

- If you arrive in the classroom and cannot locate the class seating chart, simply sketch the student desk arrangement on a sheet of typing paper and ask students to write their names in the correct location. Knowing students' names can eliminate many troublesome situations, as kids are less likely to misbehave when addressed by name. Also, if it becomes necessary to alert the regu-

lar teacher to a problem, you'll have the names handy.

- On index cards (one for every class member), write each of the chores you would like completed before you dismiss the class for the day, such as clean sink, straighten bookshelves, stack extra chairs, clean up floor, and line up desks. You may need more than one card for some of the jobs. On the remaining cards, write "silent reading." Shuffle the cards and have each student pick one. Clean up can be fun when a drawing starts it off.

- Bring a fun music tape to class. (Disney® tapes work well.) If students have a good day, let them listen to the tape during the last hour of the day. You can also play calming music while students do quiet work.

an alternative, you can come with the rewards on slips of paper and just discuss them with the students.

- Keep track of class behavior on the board in the room, awarding a plus each time the entire class is working, or erasing a plus when a problem arises. In the morning, establish with the class a reward for earning five pluses during the course of the day. Set aside the last fifteen minutes of the day to give the reward. Playing a thinking game, such as Hangman or Mastermind, makes a good, motivating reward. Here's how to play Mastermind:

Make the following chart on the board.

Choose a three-digit number, but do not tell students. (Two digits are appropriate for primary students; four digits can be used after students have practiced, or with advanced students.) Students then guess the three-digit number using the information from previous guesses on the chart. The game can also be played with words instead of numbers.

- At the beginning of the day, allow students to brainstorm motivating rewards for the class that do not require money (being dismissed a minute early, playing a learning game, listening to music, etc.). Write all of the ideas on slips of paper. Then, if the class behaves appropriately for the entire day, allow one person to draw a slip at the end of the day. Be sure to include only the ideas that you are willing to do. As

Numbers Guessed	Number of Correct Digits	Number of Digits in Correct Place
_____	_____	_____
_____	_____	_____
_____	_____	_____
_____	_____	_____

Mastermind Sample Number Game

Real number: **327**

Numbers Guessed	Number of Correct Digits	Number of Digits in Correct Place
431	1	0
125	1	1
920	1	1
720	2	1
024	1	1
727	2	2
327	3	3

Mastermind Sample Word Game

Real word: **eat**

Word Guessed	Number of Correct Letters	Number of Letters in Correct Place
see	1	0
set	2	1
sat	2	2
sad	1	1
ear	2	2
red	1	0
tea	3	0
ate	3	0
eat	3	3

- Personalize bingo for the classroom and use it as a filler, reward, or as a lesson plan in itself. Give each student a copy of the blank bingo card that follows. Then, read off (or write on overhead or board) a list of twenty-four words. Students choose any space in which to draw a picture of each word, or write the word itself. Students may place the word "free" in one box. Remind students that it is to their advantage not to look at their neighbors' cards, since both people will play bingo at the same time. Here are some ideas for bingo lists, but feel free to compile your own lists to fit current events, seasons, sports, news stories, subjects, math facts, and so on.

Thanksgiving: cornucopia, turkey, squash, mashed potatoes, orange, corn, pilgrim, stuffing, football, pumpkin, gourds, pumpkin pie, pecan pie, cranberries, rolls, relatives, whipped cream, pastry, pudding, olives, gravy, sweet potatoes, candy, leaves

School: reading, writing, math, apples, pencil, ruler, desk, chalkboard, classroom, eraser, teacher, students, bell, recess, lunch, study, music, library, PE, books, backpack, uniform, pens, stickers

When students have completed their bingo cards, call out the words in random order and have them mark the appropriate squares. Students can use candy corn, raisins, mini-marshmallows, tiddlywinks, scraps of paper, or any small objects to mark their squares. The first student to build a complete row in any direction of covered squares calls "Bingo!" to win. For variety, call different types of games such as two bingos on one card, four corners, or any other configuration.

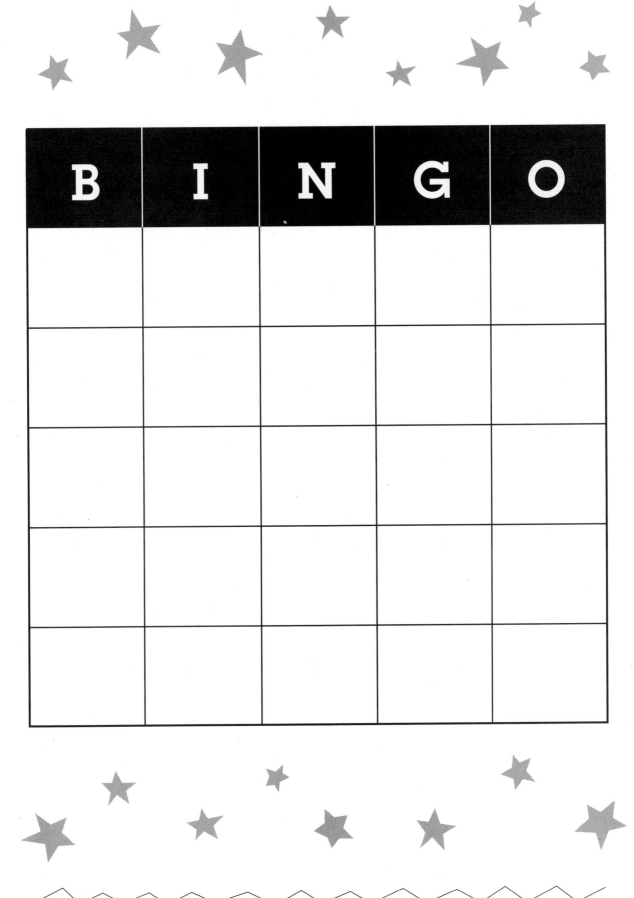

B	I	N	G	O

When Substituting Is Extended

You may be called for a substitute job that extends over a period of time. Circumstances such as injury, accident, attending a conference, or childbirth, may keep the regular teacher out of the classroom from a few days to many weeks. At these times, the rules of substituting change a bit. You'll have some new needs to address.

Classroom Rules

Since you will be in charge of the class for a longer period of time, you need to have rules with which both you and the students can live. Do not throw out basic classroom and school rules that are already established. Instead, address the small, everyday rules that keep the class on track, such as visiting the restrooms, getting drinks, sharpening pencils, raising hands to speak, and settling disputes.

Students tend to follow rules without complaint if they have had some voice in the selection process. Have a brainstorming session with the class. Ask students to share rules that they would like to see enforced while you are in charge. Remind the class that rules must be consistent with school and safety policies. List all the suggested rules on the board.

Divide the class into groups of three to five students. Pick a recorder for each group. Using the list, have each group pick two rules that are important to them. Encourage an exchange of opinions and reasons for choices.

Call the class back together and have the recorders put check marks by the chosen rules. Tally the results and implement the top four to six rules. Print them out for the class and post them in front of the room for the duration of your stay. You may tell the class that you, the teacher, reserve the right to add one rule. Now you can insert your preference into the list.

Homework Assignments

You will probably have to begin giving out homework. (Most parents expect to see assignments on a regular basis.) Here are some simple guidelines that you can follow.

Check to see if a regular homework policy exists for the school or grade level (twice a week, no homework on weekends, etc.). You do not want to violate accepted rules.

Try to make the assignments meaningful. No one likes to be stuck with "busy work." Tie the assignments into current curriculum or practice sessions for work that has already been taught (math facts, states and capitals, etc.). Students seem to enjoy enrichment work, especially if it involves hands-on activities.

Remember, homework assignments should never involve new learning that requires considerable assistance or raises too many questions to clarify the expectations. It should be an extension of the classroom work or a chance to complete unfinished assignments. No one says that homework can't be fun!

Some of the lessons in this book require preparation such as collecting leaves for an art lesson or collecting labels for a science lesson. Use homework time to have the students collect their own materials for the following day's lesson.

Getting to Know the Students

Since you will be with the class for a while, the better you get to know the students, the happier you will all be. A nice way to learn about them is to give a special assignment on the first day. Ask the class to think of important things about themselves that they might like to share with a new friend (hobbies, talents, family members, favorite food, etc.).

At home, have the students fill a brown bag or shoe box with eight to ten items that reveal something about them. Help the students by giving some examples, such as a soccer shoe, trophy, family picture, wrapper from food item, or baseball card. Put together a collection of items relating to yourself, as well. Encourage originality and

humor. If an item is too big for the bag, a drawing or picture will suffice.

On the following day, take time to share the results. You go first to set the mood. Be chatty and open. It will give the kids a chance to get to know you as well. During breaks throughout the day, let a few more students share until everyone has a turn. You will be surprised how much you will learn about the students, and how much they will learn about each other and you.

Publish the News

What did the class do while the regular teacher was away? Publish a newspaper! This fun and educational project will let the parents and teacher know what went on in the room while you, the substitute, were in command.

On the last day before you leave, take time to review the events that took place during the regular teacher's absence. Have the students brainstorm

all the things you did together, both lessons and other activities, and write the list on the board. Include funny stories and problems that you faced and solved. This will remind the students of all the learning that went on while you were together.

During writing time, divide the students into small groups. Have each group pick a different topic (choosing from the list on the board) and write a short article about the choice. Since you have planned this event ahead of time, you can ask the Room Parent to recruit a volunteer to type the articles in a newsletter format as they are finished. A student can illustrate the paper if time allows.

Send home a copy of the newspaper with each student. Remember to leave a copy on the teacher's desk as well.

Leave the Classroom Neat

We talked about cleaning the room before dismissing the students each day. The cleaning process is more involved when you are there for a period of time. Make sure everything is back in order before the regular teacher returns. If you have rearranged furniture, put it back the way it was. If you have been using art supplies, store them as you originally found them. Make sure books have been returned to the library if you checked any out.

If you complete an art project, it might be nice to hang the work on the windows or a bulletin board. It is easier for a teacher to return to the class if the room is neat and pleasant.

Welcome the Teacher Back

It is always hard for a teacher to be away from the classroom for an extended period of time. When the teacher does return, it is nice to know that he or she was missed. You can prepare the students for the teacher's return by suggesting that the class make a special gift. A "Welcome Back" banner is easy to make and all the students can sign it. Each student could write a short note or illustrate a card for the teacher. You might purchase a small treat (cookies, doughnuts, candy, etc.), and leave it for the students to share with their teacher. Kids love surprises especially if they are in on the planning.

Finally

If you do a good job as a substitute, you will be called back. Teachers are always looking for a reliable person, especially when they know that the job extends for some time. When you come prepared and knowledgeable, the students, the parents, and the regular teacher all come out winners. And that makes you a winner too!

PART II

The Lesson Plans

In the next section are lesson plans for nearly every subject area and encompassing every elementary grade. Make notes about what works as well as any adaptations you devise directly on the lesson plan. These plans should provide many days of productive learning wherever you go!

Building Vocabulary Blocks

Objective:

To use silent reading as a tool for building new vocabulary words

Teacher Preparation:

Make sure each class member has a book in his or her desk. (Books may come from home, the class library, or the school library.) You should have a book to read as well. A good role model is essential when encouraging the love of reading! You will also need paper and pencil for each student.

Instructions:

At a designated time, have each student get out a book and begin silent reading. (Right after lunch/recess or at the beginning of the reading block are good times to include this quiet activity.) As they read, students should jot down on a piece of paper any new or exciting words that they come across. At the end of the session (ten to fifteen minutes is plenty for younger students) ask the class to share their "special" words. List them on the board and discuss the meanings. Students who recognize the words can help define them. You might add a word from your book too.

Variation:

Ask students to read aloud a favorite phrase, sentence, or paragraph from their books. Stress action words and descriptive phrases. Model this exercise using a passage from your chosen book. As students get used to identifying descriptive phrases, they will begin to include these types of words in their own writing.

Story Dressing: Making a Book Jacket

Objective:

To make a book jacket illustrating the highlights of a favorite book

Teacher Preparation:

Have available a large piece of white construction paper for each student. Collect a few book jackets from published books. (The school librarian can help you get these or use some of your own covers from home.) You also will need to provide pencils and crayons or markers for writing and decoration.

Instructions:

Begin by sharing the book jackets you brought to class. Take a look at what publishers put on the front, back, and side flaps of the jackets. Ask the students to choose a favorite book for this project. Pass out the white construction paper and ask students to fold it in half lengthwise. Then fold the ends over about a quarter again to make the flaps. On the front cover, have students draw a picture of their favorite part of the story and add the title. On the back cover they should describe the main characters or plot, or give a summary of the book. On the inside front flap, students should write a sentence telling what they liked about the book. Finally, on the inside back flap, them tell a bit about themselves. (Explain to the class that this is like an author's page.)

Variation:

For younger students, read aloud a picture book prior to the activity, and have them all make book jackets for that story.

Scavenging the News

Objective:

To explore and pinpoint some of the varied information found in a newspaper using a scavenger hunt

Teacher Preparation:

Bring a number of newspapers to class. They need not be the same edition or date. Copy the scavenger hunt list that follows for each student group. You also will need to provide paper, scissors, pencils, and glue.

Instructions:

Divide the students into teams of two to four, depending on the number of newspapers available. Give each team a newspaper and a copy of the scavenger hunt list. Students should find the requested items and then cut out and glue them on a piece of paper.

Variation:

Within each group, students can work individually, sharing newspapers. Discuss strategies for finding various items. (Did the group divide the list, or randomly look for the answers?) Adapt the list if some of the items are too easy or difficult to find.

Scavenging the News, *cont.*

Scavenger Hunt List

Directions: Find, cut out, and glue on a sheet of paper one sample of each item listed. You may use words, pictures, or both. Be sure to number your cutouts.

1. A number greater than one hundred

2. A person wearing glasses

3. An animal (Next to this item, list the names of the people in your group who have ever touched this type of animal.)

4. A sports headline. Draw a picture to illustrate it.

5. The price of a used car

6. A vehicle other than an automobile

7. A compound word (such as houseboat or notebook)

8. The name of a city in your state

9. A number between five and twenty

10. A toy or piece of sporting equipment

11. The name of a movie that is playing at a local theater

12. A happy word (such as smile or friendly)

13. A number between twenty and fifty

14. The name of a country other than the United States of America

15. The high temperature of a large city

Chaining a Story

Objective:

To create a short story using cause and effect

Teacher Preparation:

Prepare a set of index cards for each student with the first and sixth sentences as described in the instructions. Students can receive the same set of sentences. It is fun to see different approaches to the same situation. You will also need paper, pencils, and scissors.

Instructions:

Explain to students that one event may often cause a chain of events. Choose a current news story familiar to students. Discuss the previous event(s) that caused the current event to occur. (The volcano caused people to move, which caused overcrowding in the shelters, and so on.) Hand each student an index card with a beginning sentence (sentence one) and an ending sentence (sentence six). The task is to write the four sentences between the first and sixth sentence so that the story makes sense, flows sequentially, and gets the reader from sentence one to sentence six in a logical manner.

Chaining a Story, *cont.*

Sample Sentences:

1. Fires burned in Montserrat Monday as the island's volcano flowed into the city of Plymouth.

6. All residents were rescued in boats and were unharmed.

1. My pumpkin got smashed by a falling tree.

6. We went to the zoo together, and the zookeeper gave me a kangaroo.

1. The chair collapsed at my sister's wedding.

6. The jazz band pulled my sister out of a tuba.

1. D.A.R.E. officers attended a local elementary school to give prizes for the drug abuse poster contest.

6. The students were able to evacuate the gym in only two minutes.

After the students create their stories, they should make a "chain" of six shapes that are related to the story (volcano, boats, pumpkins, tubas, etc.) and write each sentence in one of the shapes. See sample below. These stories are fun to display on the classroom wall!

Variations:
- Students can work in cooperative groups of two or three to compose their stories.
- Have students act out or perform their sequences. Encourage humor and originality.

My pumpkin got smashed by a falling tree.

The tree rolled right next to a school bus.

The bus swerved to avoid the tree.

A cute boy named Ken grabbed me so I missed getting hit.

We went to the zoo together, and the zookeeper gave me a kangaroo.

29

Root Monsters

Objective:

To combine common Latin prefixes and root words and create body parts for a monster

Teacher Preparation:

Prepare a list of prefixes and root words. Prior to the lesson, write the list on the board or overhead, or make a copy for each student. You may also have the students take notes while you read the list aloud. It is helpful to create a few sample monsters to share with the class. You will also need paper and a pencil for each student.

Instructions:

Review with students the meaning of the terms *prefix* and *root word*. Then write the words *tricycle*, *tripod*, and *triangle* on the board. Ask the students the meaning of each word. What do all three objects have in common? (They all have three of something—three wheels, three legs, three angles.) Review the following lists of prefixes and root words with students, using them in common words when possible. (What is a *microscope*? Can anyone put together the prefix and root word to tell me what *pachyderm* means?)

Prefixes:

uni - one

du, bi - two

tri - three

quadri - four

penta - five

hexa, sex - six

hepta - seven

octo - eight

ennea - nine

deca - ten

demi, hemi - half

pachy - thick

hetero - different

homeo - similar

lipo - fat

macro - large

micro - small

mero - part

multi, poly - many

pan - all

scoli - crooked

cerule - blue

chlor - green

blanc, alb - white

Root Words:

caput - head

manus - hand

nasus - nose

oculus - eye

ped - foot

corp - body

oss - bone

digit - finger

maxil - jaw

brac - arm

cerc, caud - tail

stom - mouth

tops - face

cera, corn - horn

derm - skin

equ, hipp - horse

sengel - snail

saur - lizard

Root Monsters, *cont.*

Ask a student to combine one prefix with a root word (*Heptaoculus* = seven-eyed). Select another student to combine a different prefix with a root word (*Macrocaud* = large-tailed). Ask the class to sketch a seven-eyed, large-tailed monster.

Have each student create a monster, combining prefixes with root words. Remind them that these words are the names of the monsters, so the first letter of each prefix should be capitalized (Heptaoculus Macrocaud).

Variations:

- Students may combine more pairs of prefixes and root words to make their monsters more specific.

  Example: Macrocaput Microstom Triped Quadribrac (large-headed, small-mouthed, three-footed, four-armed monster)

- Use the completed monsters as flashcards to review the meanings of the prefixes and root words studied.

Grades 4–6

Classifying Our Reading

Objective:

To use newspaper stories and ads to classify subject areas

Teacher Preparation:

Collect a set of short newspaper stories, columns, and ads for each student. If you will be returning to the class the following day, students can find their own articles as a homework assignment. Encourage them to pick a topic that interests them.

Instructions:

Pass out clippings randomly to the students, or have them get out their own selection. Ask them to scan their piece and decide on a subject or category that it might fit, such as sports, food, weather, history, health, foreign country. Have a student share his or her article and a suggested category. Write the response on the board. See if anyone else has a clipping that might fit into the category. Have other students share. After you have written a few categories on the board, ask if any student has a clipping that might fit into more than one category. Students should be allowed to explain their decisions. Now have students write down as many categories as they can think of for their individual articles or ads. Use this exercise to discuss cross-referencing.

Variation:

Use the newspaper pictures instead of articles. This will make it easier for younger students who do not have enough reading skills to decode the copy.

Adding the Punctuation Mark

Objective:

To practice using correct punctuation marks by encouraging each student to add his or her choice of ending punctuation to given sentences

Teacher Preparation:

Collect a sampling of sentences that end in periods, question marks, and exclamation points. Cut up pieces of white construction or typing paper into four equal parts. (Each student will need three pieces.) You will also need a black crayon or marker for each student.

Instructions:

Pass out three sections of paper to each student. Using a black crayon or marker, have each student put a period on one piece of paper, a question mark on the second, and an exclamation point on the third. (You should draw the symbols on the board.) As you read aloud a sentence, each student decides which punctuation mark is appropriate to end the sentence. When you say, "Show me," each student holds up one of his or her cards.

Variation:

Have each student pick only one of the three punctuation cards and put the other two away. Then, when you read a sentence, only the students holding the cards with the required punctuation marks respond.

Bottled Note

Objective:

To motivate student creativity by using a visual prop to begin the story-writing process

Teacher Preparation:

Prepare a bottle with a rolled-up message inside. Make the message funny, mysterious, or challenging. You will also need writing paper and a pencil or pen for each student.

Instructions:

Show the bottle with the paper rolled inside to the class. Ask the students to think about the following questions: Who put the message in the bottle? Where did the bottle originate? Who found the bottle? Where was the bottle found?

Be sure to get lots of answers to the questions. Write the responses on the board or use an overhead projector.

After you have given everyone a chance to respond, discuss some of the answers. A child that couldn't think of an original answer might be able to add information to someone else's response.

Pass out writing paper. Ask each class member to write a paragraph (or short story) about the bottle and its message. Encourage use of the information that is written on the board. Students may add any descriptive details that they choose. Model the assignment to help students get started.

Variation:

Divide the students into small groups to write a story together. One member of each group should be assigned to be the recorder. Stories can be illustrated individually or by the group.

Recognizing Parts of Speech

Objective:

To help primary students identify nouns and verbs by using examples

Teacher Preparation:

Gather a set of newspaper or magazine pages, one for each member of the class. (Larger print words from headlines, cutlines, and ads are easier for younger students to work with.) You also will need glue, scissors, and writing paper for each student.

Instructions:

Introduce the meaning of noun (the name of a person, a place, or a thing) and verb (an action word). Practice naming nouns that can be found in the classroom. Brainstorm a list of verbs or ways to show action.

Pass out the pages of the newspaper or magazine, glue, scissors, and sheets of typing or notebook paper. Ask the students to make two columns, one for nouns and one for verbs, on their papers. Students should begin clipping out nouns or verbs and gluing them to their papers in the correct column. After a few minutes, share some of the responses, correcting any mistakes that might occur. Encourage students to check with a partner or you if they are

not sure of a certain word. Younger students can concentrate on one part of speech.

Variation:

For older students, you might introduce adjectives as well. Have students find a noun and then look for words that describe the noun.

Grades 1–3

Creating a Spelling Puzzle

Objective:

To help students practice their spelling words by creating a puzzle using the weekly spelling list

Teacher Preparation:

Make one copy of the Spelling Puzzle Grid that follows for each member of the class. You will need to make sure each student has a copy of the current spelling list. Additionally, each student will need a pencil.

Instructions:

Pass out a Spelling Puzzle Grid to each student (see grid on page 90). Have students write each of the words in the grid, either vertically, diagonally, or horizontally, backward or forward, and fill in the remaining spaces with random letters. Have students exchange papers and find the hidden spelling words. Be sure students double-check the spelling of each word after they place it in their puzzles. No one wants to work on a puzzle with misspelled words.

Variation:

Before you start working on the puzzle, go over the spelling list. Look for words with double letters and point them out to the students. Also look for little words within the larger words. Making the children aware of certain patterns will help them spell the words correctly when they begin work on the puzzle.

Writing a Will

Objective:

To practice humorous writing by con-
cocting an imaginary will for an imaginary person

Teacher Preparation:

Each student will need writing paper
and a pencil or pen.

Instructions:

Ask students to choose a silly name
for their fictitious will writer, such as Suzy
Snowcone. Then have them make a list
of the silly person's prized possessions
(cherry syrup, ice machine, etc.). Share
this example on the board, if necessary.

Now students are ready to prepare
their characters' wills. Encourage
humor. Students can have a lot of fun
with this activity. Share wills aloud—it's
half the fun of this assignment.

Variation:

Instead of writing wills, for imaginary people, have students pick
famous people (George Washington;
Martin Luther King, Jr.; Walt Disney;
Michael Jordan; Oprah Winfrey; etc.)
and write fictitious wills for them.

"I, Suzy Snowcone, leave my cherry syrup to . . . . "

Poetry with a "P"

Objective:

To help students build interest in and appreciation of poetry by having them write alliterative poems

Teacher Preparation:

Go to the school library and find some children's poetry books. (Elementary students particularly enjoy *Where the Sidewalk Ends* and *Light in the Attic* by Shel Silverstein.) You also will need writing paper, plain white paper, pencils and pens, and colored pencils for each student.

Instructions:

Read aloud a few selections of poetry from your chosen books. Be a good role model by reading enthusiastically. Encourage any class member who has a verse memorized to share it at this time.

Now assign each student one letter of the alphabet. (More than one pupil can share a particular letter.) Ask students to list as many nouns, adjectives, verbs, and adverbs that begin with their assigned letters as possible. Once a list has been compiled, they should compose phrases beginning with their letters.

Example:

Beautiful bud

Blowing in the breeze,

Brave little flower

Beckoning me.

Borrowed from nature

Bold and free,

Beautiful bud

Belonging to me.

When students complete their alliterative poems, share some of them aloud with the class. Then let students print them on white paper and add a decorative border with colored pencils using their letters as a design motif.

Variation:

If the students show some interest in poetry, you might introduce couplets, two lines of verse that rhyme. This is another easy pattern to duplicate. You will be surprised how even reluctant students will turn on to poetry.

Illustrating Idioms

Objective:

To help students understand the value of idioms in daily speech

Teacher Preparation:

Each student will need a piece of plain white paper, a pen or pencil, and crayons or markers.

Instructions:

Explain the meaning of the word *idiom* to the class. (An expression or phrase that cannot be understood from the ordinary meaning of words in it.) Tell them how hard it is for nonnative English speakers to understand all the "figures of speech" that Americans use in their daily lives. Write several examples on the board. (Hold your tongue. She was angry and blew a fuse. It was raining cats and dogs. My dad is all thumbs in the garden.) Ask the students to add to your list. If you have trouble thinking of idioms, check the school library for help. The stories in the scenes of *Amelia Bedelia* (by Peggy Parish) make wonderful use of idioms.

Have each student select one idiom from the board or one of their own choosing. They should illustrate the meaning of the phrase both literally and as intended as a figure of speech. Be sure to have them write the idiom somewhere on the paper. This activity would be fun to display on the bulletin board.

Variation:

Have the students act out their idioms and see if the rest of the class can guess what they are portraying.

Group Stories

Objective:

To help students share talents by writing group stories (This process relieves the pressure from students who have difficulty writing a story from scratch)

Teacher Preparation:

Collect enough pictures from books, magazines, newspapers, postcards, and so on, for everyone in class. Choose pictures of active people rather than scenery. You will also need paper and a pen or pencil for each student.

Instructions:

Divide the class into groups of four or five students. Have each group find a space on the floor and sit in a circle. Each member of the group needs paper, pencil, something to write on, and one of the pictures. To begin the assignment, ask students to write the first three or four sentences of a story, using their pictures as visual guides. They then pass the stories and pictures clockwise to their neighbor who adds three or four sentences to the story. Students continue passing the stories until everyone receives his or her story back. The story's originator then writes the ending of the story. Share some of the stories aloud.

Variation:

Use the stories to start a discussion about the writing process. Ask students questions about their stories. Did the story turn out the way you expected it to when you started writing? Did it take any unexpected turns? Do you enjoy writing as a group or do you prefer to write individual stories? What are some of the advantages of working in a team? of working alone?

Working Word Problems

Objective:

To help students analyze story problems even when their reading skills are minimal

Teacher Preparation:

Prepare a list of simple story problems that require the student to determine the operation, work the problem, and disregard unnecessary information. (See sample problems that follow.)

Instructions:

Have students get out a piece of scratch paper and pencil. Tell them that they can take notes, but you will only give out the information twice so they must be quiet listeners. State the problems clearly. Speak slowly so the class has time to absorb the information. Use as few words as possible.

Sample problems:

4 bikes, 2 balls, 1 bat, 3 kites
How many toys? (10 toys)

5 babies, 2 cats, 1 dog, 4 cars
How many legs? (22 legs)

3 fish, 4 puppies, 2 books, 5 birds
How many pets? (12 pets)

3 boats, 1 car, 2 bikes
How many wheels? (8 wheels)

Work some problems together as a class before expecting the children to work on their own. Make the problems progressively harder as the class better understands the format.

Variation:

Have the students make up their own story problems. You might add problems with multiple operations (add, then subtract) as you go along.

Helping Hands

Objective:

To help students practice math facts using a visual aid

Teacher Preparation:

Each student will need white paper and a pencil and access to scissors.

Instructions:

Pass out a piece of white paper to each student. Ask the class to trace the outline of their hands and then cut out the drawings. Have them write any five numbers from one to nine on the fingers. Remind them that they should not write the numbers in any order. Now offer some math exercises, using the numbers on the hands. Example: Find the sum of all the numbers on the hand. Add a given number to each of the finger numbers. Add the first, third, and fifth numbers and then subtract the second and fourth numbers from the sum. Students can number and then record their answers on the back of the hand. Have them exchange hands with a partner to correct the work.

Variation:

Have younger children trace their hands on the paper but leave the fingers blank. Then give simple oral problems to the class and ask the children to record their answers on the fingers. Using both sides of the cutout shapes allows room for ten math problems.

Graphing Birthdays

Objective:

To help students understand bar graphs by recording the number of classroom birthdays that occur in each of the twelve months

Teacher Preparation:

None

Instructions:

Bar graphs are just one kind of graph that students will have to learn to read. To pique their interest in a fun way, record on a bar graph how many birthdays fall in each month. To begin the study, ask students to predict which month will have the most birthdays. Ask them to write down their guesses to compare to the actual results.

Pick a recorder to come to the board. He or she will tally marks as you call roll, asking for each child's birth month as you do. The recorder totals the tally marks. Now draw a bar graph on the board or chart paper, writing the months of the year along the horizontal axis and the numbers one through ten on the vertical axis. Draw a bar representing the correct number of birthdays in each month. How many students correctly predicted the highest month?

Variation:

Instead of drawing an ordinary bar graph, students could use pictures of cakes, candles, balloons, or other birthday symbols above the months on the graph.

String Measurement

Objective:

To give students practice measuring in centimeters and inches

Teacher Preparation:

Cut a length of string (approximately fifteen inches) for each student. Make sure rulers are available if class members do not have their own. Rulers should have both centimeters and inches marked. You also will need scratch paper and pencils.

Instructions:

Hand out a piece of string to each student. Tell them to use the string to help them measure. Give them the following directions.

1. Wrap the string around an object to be measured, such as an ankle.

2. Pinch the string on the long end to hold your place where the measurement stops.

3. Still pinching the string, lay the string along the ruler to check the circumference of the ankle, the length of the string from beginning to the pinched part, in inches and centimeters.

Students should soon realize that one inch equals more than two centimeters. To extend the activity, have students estimate a measurement in both systems before taking the measurement.

Variations:

- After students practice measuring their own body parts, they can find other things to measure. For instance, ask them to measure at least five different school supplies (books, pencil, eraser, chalk, paper, notebook, etc.).

- Ask the students how they can measure a larger object, such as a desk or chair, using the same piece of string. This will get the class to use some problem-solving skills.

Restaurant Math

Objective:

To give students a chance to work with money story problems using a restaurant menu

Teacher Preparation:

Before class begins, write up a fake menu on a blank overhead transparency, or use the one that follows. Be sure to include the kinds of food that kids like to eat (hamburgers, fries, ice cream, etc.). Add prices for each item. If you want to make the math more challenging, do not round out the prices to tens and hundreds. For example, make a price $2.29 instead of $2.00 or $2.30. For fun, you might add some unusual items such as liver burger or carrot shake. Each student will need scratch paper and a pencil.

Instructions:

Tell students to have pencils and scratch paper ready. Show the prepared transparency on the overhead projector. (Or copy and distribute the worksheet and menu on the following pages.)

Give the students directions using the menu. For example:

- How much does it cost to purchase a hamburger, fries, and shake?

- Add up the two most expensive items on the menu. How much do they cost?

- Subtract the least expensive item from the most expensive item.

- How much does it cost to buy three orders of fries and two shakes?

- Choose a full meal for each member of your family. How much does it cost to feed the group?

- Subtract the cost of a milk shake from the cost of a hamburger.

Variations:

- Use the menu prices to practice rounding. For example, round each price to the nearest dollar.

- Have students write their own story problems using the data on the menu. Share problems with the class.

- For older children, extend the lesson by having them compute the tax on their meal and/or have them compute the tip.

Delicious Diner Menu

Entrees

Hamburger	. . . .$2.29	Ostrich Burger	. . . .$4.39
Cheeseburger	. . . . . .$2.49	Liver Burger	. . . .$2.19
Chicken Sandwich	. . .$3.39	Shark Steak	. . . .$6.29
Chicken Salad	. . . . . .$4.25	Chef Salad	. . . .$4.25
Turkey Sandwich	. . . .$4.00	Chicken Strips	. . . . . .$4.50

Side Orders

French Fries	. . . .$1.25	Deep-Fried Beets	. . . . .$2.29
Onion Rings	. . . .$2.29	Split-Pea Soup	. . . . . .$2.99
Squash Soup	. . . .$2.99	Fresh Fruit	. . . .$2.29

Beverages and Desserts

Soda Pop	. . . .$1.19	Strawberry Sundae	. . .$2.59
Carrot Milk Shake	. . . .$1.79	Rhubarb Pie	. . . .$2.69
Iced Tea	. . . .$1.19	Mud Pie	. . . .$3.29
Coffee	. . . .$1.09	Chocolate Cake	. . . . .$2.99

Delicious Diner Worksheet

How much would the following items cost?

1. A hamburger, fries, and a carrot milk shake _____

2. The two most expensive items on the menu _____

3. Two orders of chicken strips _____

4. A liver burger, two orders of onion rings, and coffee _____

5. All of the dessert items _____

Find the answers to the following problems.

6. Subtract the least expensive item on
the menu from the most expensive item _____

7. What is the cost of three fries and two split-pea soups?_____

8. Choose a full meal for each member of your family.
How much will it cost to feed the group? _____

9. Design the healthiest meal you can.
How much will the meal cost?_____

Your menu:

_____

_____

_____

10. If you could eat a full meal of whatever you want from the menu,
how much would it cost?_____

Your menu:

_____

_____

_____

Playing with Names

Objective:

To practice addition, subtraction, multiplication, and division using student names

Teacher Preparation:

Each student needs a piece of black paper and a pencil.

Instructions:

Start this math activity by having each student write the alphabet in one column on a piece of paper and then number the letters: A=1, B=2, C=3, D=4, and so on. Ask the students to write their preferred first names at the top of the paper. (Each must use this name during the exercise. A nickname is fine, as long as they stay with it.) Tell the students to find the value of their names. Does the longest name guarantee the highest value? Estimate which letter is going to be used the most. Will it be a consonant or a vowel? How would multiplication figure in the math? (If there are double letters in a name.)

Now have the students write their full names on their papers (first, middle, and last). Find the value of each of the three names. Ask who has the name with the most points? least points? Total all three names and divide by three to find the average value. Ask for a volunteer to work his or her math on the board. The class can then proofread together. If students need help with the math, assign partners to proof and correct with them.

Variation:

Using the same alphabet value chart, do quick mental math problems using objects in the room. Start with short objects and then move to longer ones. Add subtraction problems for a challenge. Example: subtract "desk" from "clock." Allow the students to keep written notes if they cannot keep the information in their heads.

Structuring Geometry

Objective:

To learn about geometric shapes by building them out of toothpicks

Teacher Preparation:

Bring a box of toothpicks for this project. (Rounded ones work better than flattened ones.) Check with the office for a supply of clay. Have rulers available for the class to use.

Instructions:

Students may work in groups or individually. Give each group or student a bunch of toothpicks and a piece of clay. Ask them to form simple geometric shapes such as squares, rectangles, parallelograms, triangles, and rhombuses (an equilateral parallelogram).

Now challenge the class to build the tallest structure possible, and then the widest. Discuss the strategies they can use to increase the strength of the structures.

Variation:

Specify stricter parameters such as using only twelve toothpicks, making five points touching the desk, or thinking of and making another geometric shape. Allow enough time for students to get creative with their designs.

Humanizing Fractions

Objective:

To help students visualize the concept of fractions by "role-playing" fractional relationships

Teacher Preparation:

Each student will need scrap paper and a pencil.

Instructions:

Appoint a recorder to work at the board. Ask the rest of the class to work on scratch paper at their seats. Have twelve students come to the front of the room. Encourage them to be creative in their responses. Tell the group to form the fraction one-half. (Six students could stand, and six kneel; half could clap and half not.) Have the recorder write the fraction "6 out of 12 = 1/2." Using the same group of students, repeat the process with thirds, fourths, and sixths. Choose ten students and repeat the procedure, using halves, fifths, and tenths.

Variations:

- Ask a single student to come to the front of the room and demonstrate a fraction using only body parts. (Hold up seven fingers and fold three under; swing one arm and hold the other arm still.) Again, encourage creativity.

- Have all students work at their seats. How many fractions can they use to describe objects they see around the room? (How many windows have curtains?)

Classifying Crayons

Objective:

To learn the technique of classifying and identifying multiple attributes using crayons

Teacher Preparation:

Make sure all students either have their own box of crayons or provide a container of crayons from which students can grab a handful. You will also need scratch paper and pens or pencils.

Instructions:

Ask students to lay their collection of crayons on their desks. Students should separate the crayons into different categories. Have them record the groupings on scratch paper before they start a new category. Challenge them to find five different ways to sort or classify the crayons. For example, they might divide into dark colors and light colors, with paper and without paper, long and short, with points and without points, and fat and skinny.

Remind the students that when they classify or sort, they should look for similarities and differences in shape, size, color, texture, weight, and other shared characteristics.

Variation:

Ask the students to think about other collections that they might have at home that would make good specimens for classifying (coins, jars, buttons, stamps, marbles, books, etc.).

Scavenging for Nature's Treasures

Objective:

To discover nature's gifts on a scientific scavenger hunt

Teacher Preparation:

Have a small plastic bag available for each class member. Prepare a scavenger list of simple objects that can be found on the playground and make a copy for each student. A sample list follows on p. 53.

Instructions:

Tell the students that they will be going on a very special hunt and give each a small plastic bag and a list. Tell them to find an example of each category on their list. (It might be a good idea to pair off younger students so that they can compare notes with a partner.) Encourage students to be creative as they interpret the items. Go over the list and answer any questions. Tell students that you will be available during the activity to assist.

Before students leave the classroom, set outdoor boundaries. (They must stay within your sight; go only as far as the swings; etc.) Carry a whistle so you can signal when it is time for students to return to the classroom. Establish a "waiting place" for students who complete the assignment ahead of the others.

Scavenging for Nature's Treasures, *cont.*

A Sample List:

- something with a rough edge

- a green object

- something an animal could eat

- something that is yellow, brown, black, red, blue, etc.

- a fuzzy object, hard object, soft object, etc.

- something you could write with

- something to build a nest

- an object that reflects

- where a bug could live

When the hunt is completed, have the students return to their desks and lay out the collected objects. Take time to share the treasures and hear the students' explanations of their choices.

Variations:

- Ask the students to think of one more item that would fit each category. Can they add items to the original list?

- Try a classroom scavenger hunt, looking for items that can be found indoors. (This is a good alternative during undesirable weather.)

Me and
My Shadow

Objective:

To observe and measure shadows caused by the sun at various times of the day

Teacher Preparation:

Have rulers and/or yardsticks available for measuring. You also will need note pads and pencils for each pair to record their data.

Instructions:

Begin by brainstorming all the ideas the children have about shadows and what causes them. Tell them that a shadow is the rough image cast by an object blocking rays of illumination. Talk about different light sources (sun, lamp, projector, etc.) that can cause shadows to form. Ask the students if they think shadows are always the same size. When would shadows be longer? shorter? Record the information before doing the experiment.

Choose three different times during the school day when the class is with you. (Work around specialist times.) Pair off the students and head outside to seek the sun. Ask one of the pair to stand blocking the sun, while the other partner measures the shadow. Be sure the students record their data. Repeat the process twice more during the day.

After the students have collected measurements at three different times of the day, share the information. Why does the shadow change at different times of the day? Discuss the fact that the sun changes position as the day progresses.

Variations:

- Talk about a sundial and how it measures the angle of the sun by casting a shadow on a special dial. Have a student look up sundial in the encyclopedia, or find a book about sundials in the library.

- Using the light from the overhead projector, experiment with different shadow images that can be formed. Some students may like to try shaping animals or birds.

Star Struck

Objective:

To get the class interested in astronomy by having students study constellations

Teacher Preparation:

Look up constellations in the encyclopedia and run a copy of some of the familiar stellar groups (Cygnus the Swan, Leo the Lion, Draco the Dragon, or Ursa Major the Great Bear.) Several books in the school library should give you information.

You also will need white paper and a pencil (or dark blue or black construction paper and foil stars) for each student or group to illustrate constellations.

Instructions:

Explain to the class that there are more than eighty star groups or *constellations*, each resembling and named after mythological characters, inanimate objects, and animals.

Assign a constellation to each student or group of students. More than one person can have the same star group. Have the class draw the arrangements of stars on pieces of white paper. (If you have foil stars to use, they can be applied to dark blue or black construction paper.)

When the drawings are completed, have each student write a creative paragraph explaining the meaning of his or her particular constellation.

Variation:

Once the class has studied some of the mythology surrounding the constellations, have each student make up an original star formation, give it a name, and explain the myth that surrounds it.

Inventive Minds

Objective:

To invent a machine that performs an undesirable chore

Teacher Preparation:

You might prepare an invention of your own to set the mood for this activity. Each student will need a piece of lined and unlined paper, a pencil, and a pen.

Instructions:

Ask the students to make a list of chores that they hate to do. Then they should select one and invent a machine to do the job. Students should keep a sheet to record the following data: What is the name of the invention? What materials are needed to build it? How many working parts does it have? Briefly describe the invention.

Students can work in pairs to come up with a creation. (Sometimes it is easier when a partner is involved.) Once they have completed the written work, the partners should draw a simple picture or diagram to show how their invention works. Conclude the lesson with an "Invention Fair." Each partnership stands in front of the class and presents their project. Allow time for fellow students to ask the inventors questions. Encourage humor and lots of creativity.

Wishy-Washy Dishwasher

Variation:

Give each class member or team a piece of "junk" and ask them how they could recycle it into a usable commodity. (A paper cup could become a bird feeder, coffee scoop, paper-clip holder, etc.)

Reading the Label

Objective:

To help students understand the nutritional value of foods by learning to read labels

Teacher Preparation:

Collect a classroom set of labels taken from cans, jars, bottles, and packaged foods. (If you soak a glued label in warm water, you can usually remove it without tearing.)

Instructions:

Before you begin this lesson, talk about TV commercials that relate to food items. Tell them about one of your favorite food ads. Then ask the class to share some of their favorite ads about food. Begin the discussion with questions like—What catches your attention in a favorite commercial? Is the advertiser always honest in presenting the food? What tricks do ad agencies use to make food appear more appetizing? (They might enhance the color, size, or shape.)

Pass out a label to each student. Ask them to find the following information: How many servings in the container? How many calories in one serving? What is the total fat content? Is there cholesterol in the product? How much sodium does it contain? How are ingredients listed on the label? (They are listed in order of proportion, with the most plentiful item listed first.) Talk about the importance of reading labels in order to become healthy shoppers.

Variation:

Have the students design labels for healthy foods that they would like to package. Have them write slogans to sell their products.

Compass Cruising

Objectives:

To practice using compass directions by locating student drawings on a grid and to encourage good listening skills

Teacher Preparation:

Run a copy of the grid that follows. After students have completed their drawings in the blank squares, you will need to photocopy a classroom set of grids.

Instructions:

Pass the blank grid around the room and have each student draw a picture in one of the spaces. Depending on class size, some students or you may have to draw more than one picture. Stress simplicity and that students may not duplicate pictures.

Make copies of the grid and give one to each student. Begin by giving simple directions and then work up to more difficult challenges. For example, tell the students to start at the compass rose and move three squares south, two squares west, and one square north and then identify their location.

Variation:

Once your students have practiced using the cardinal directions, add intercardinal directions to the compass rose: northwest, southeast, and so on. Now you can give more challenging directions such as move southeast two squares. Where are you now?

Allow students to work out their own directions and present them to the class. Make sure they have a destination in mind before they start writing directions.

Compass Cruising Grid

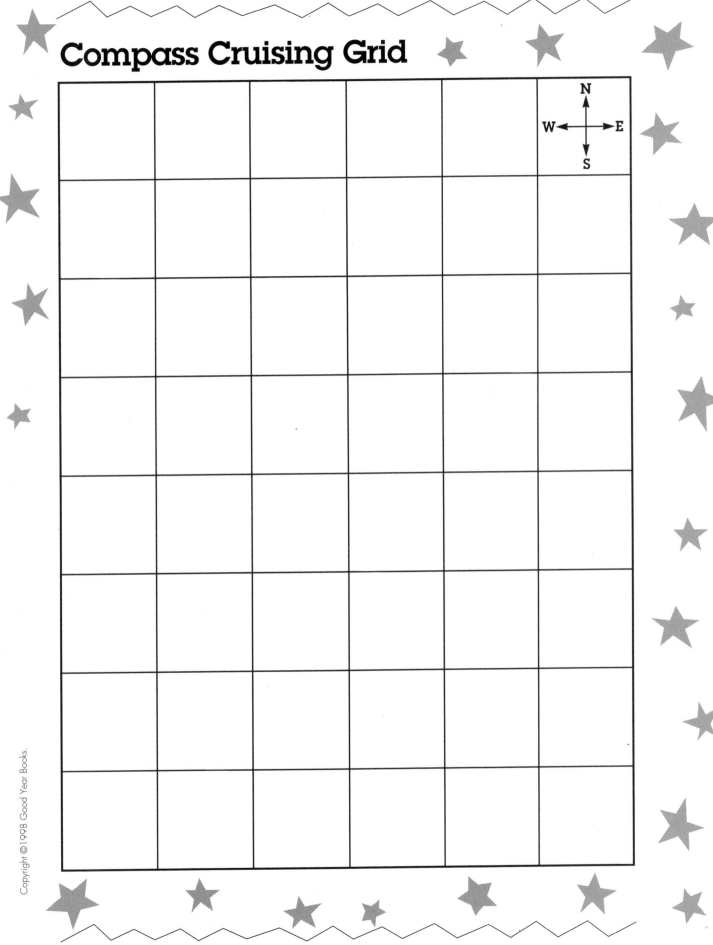

Fun with Mapping

Objective:

To introduce mapping and making a map key by having students map out their own classroom

Teacher Preparation:

Provide a piece of white typing paper (11 x 14 inches, if possible) for each class member. White construction paper also works. Each student will need a pencil.

Instructions:

Tell the students that they are going to be drawing maps of their classroom. First, they'll make a list on scratch paper of all the things in the room to be included on the map (flag, student desks, teacher desk, sink, art cart, closet, etc.). Remind the students that they cannot include everything so they should concentrate on important items. Write a compilation list on the board or overhead.

Once you have completed the list, decide on a symbol to represent each item (a small square for a student desk, a large square for the teacher's desk, a circle for the stool, etc.). Have two students count the number of student desks so you will know how many to include.

Fun with Mapping, *cont.*

Pass out the white paper to the students and ask them to draw the four walls of the room, mark front and back, and add doors, windows, and any large items hanging on walls (chalkboard, coat hooks, etc.). Using the symbols that the class has decided upon, have students lay out the furnishings on their maps. They can either map the actual classroom layout or be creative and design their own.

In one corner of the map, they should place a rectangle large enough to hold the symbols they have used. Explain that this addition is called a *key* or *legend* and helps someone read the map. (If you have a sample map, share its key with the class.)

Variation:

Add a compass rose with the four cardinal and four intercardinal directions to the maps. Ask the students directional questions, using the maps as reference: If you are at the side door, what direction would you walk to get to the sink? What direction would you walk to get from your seat to the teacher's desk? What object is southwest of the flag? Students can try making up their own questions.

Westward Go the Wagons

Objective:

To help students understand the courage and daring of the early pioneers who left their homes to brave the new frontier and build a better life for their families (They had to make many choices about supplies and furnishings, for the journey was difficult and the space was limited.)

Teacher Preparation:

Before you begin the lesson, go over some of the important challenges that pioneer families faced. Travel was slow and difficult. They gave up the comforts of civilization to head for the little-known West. They fought off Indian attacks and shot wild animals for food. They crossed thick forests, high mountains, lonely prairies, and long stretches of desert. They went by wagon, horseback, and on foot. Life was not easy on the trail. Ask students to share hardships they might have learned about from books, television, or movies. Students will need a pen or pencil and scrap paper for this activity.

Westward Go the Wagons, *cont.*

Instructions:

Begin by setting the scene for the students:

> You and your family have just arrived in Independence, Missouri. The family consists of you, your brother and sister, and your mom and dad. The year is 1850. You are going to go by covered wagon all the way to California.

> Wagon space is limited. You can only take a few items with you. What supplies would you include? Make a list of twenty things that you would bring. (Remember, you will need water, food, ammunition, and other necessities.)

After lists are completed, have students prioritize their choices, numbering them from 1 to 20. Now have students pair off. Drawing from both lists, the pair must decide together what are the top ten choices to bring.

Ask for volunteers to share their lists. The class can ask questions and challenge any items. When challenged, the partners must explain why they put those items on their list.

Variations:

- After hearing various students share their lists, have each class member revise his or her own list. What items did they add to the list? What articles did they scratch? What are five items you would they like to take but can't? What modern convenience would they miss the most?

- With younger students, prepare the supply list together as a class. Prioritize choices during a classroom discussion.

Travel Guide

Objective:

To acquaint students with their community and its resources

Teacher Preparation:

For this project you will need white typing or construction paper, pen, and crayons or colored pencils for each student. If possible, collect and share real travel brochures with the class as examples.

Instructions:

Explain to students that they are going to run a travel agency. Their first assignment is to put together a brochure selling their own city, town, or community. To interest outsiders in their area, they will need to emphasize local points of interest.

Make a list on the board of local features that the students should consider. Have the class add to the list. You should include such items as local schools, parks, places of worship, industries, and tourist attractions. What centers of interest are located nearby (colleges or universities, shopping centers, etc.)? Are there facilities for hunting, fishing, or hiking? Are you close to lakes or mountains? Be sure to consider natural views that would enhance the area. This brainstorming session will give the class a chance to visualize and get reacquainted with their own hometown. (If a student is new to the class, he or she can use a former home for the project.)

Since the list will be too long to handle in one brochure, have the students zero in on one or two of their favorite attractions. Pass out the paper and have them fold it in half. On the front cover, design a logo and a slogan for the town. Use the two inside pages to describe special attractions. On the back cover list the name of the travel agency and person to contact to get more information. Encourage creativity!

Variation:

This same idea can be used for other locations as well. If the class is studying the United States, have students pick a state other than their own to research. Or, have students pick a favorite vacation site (Disneyland, Yellowstone National Park, Mount Rainier, Washington, D.C., etc.) and design a travel brochure for this place. Be sure to have them put together a list of special features before they decide which attractions to present.

Mapping My Room

Objective:

To give students a chance to practice mapping skills by laying out blueprints of their own bedrooms

Teacher Preparation:

Have available a piece of white paper and a pencil for each student. (You may want to have students do a rough draft on notebook paper before transferring their plans to a heavier paper such as construction or tagboard.)

Instructions:

Ask the students to visualize their bedrooms. On scratch paper they should jot down familiar landmarks such as large pieces of furniture. Have them start the map by roughing out the four walls of the room and adding marks for the door and windows. They should indicate whether the doors swing in or out. They should then sketch in the bed, chest, dresser, closet, and other features. If they want, they can add decorative items such as curtains, pictures, lamps, and so on.

Although they are not drawing their rooms to scale, remind them that they should consider the relationships of space and size and try to draw the fur-

nishings accordingly. (For example, the bed would be about five times the length of the chest.)

Variation:

Read a chapter from a storybook and have students draw maps to fit the setting of the story. Be sure to share a book that includes lots of details. Ask the school librarian for suggestions. He or she might be able to recommend a book that features a map already drawn to give the students an example to follow. Winnie-the-Pooh books often have a map of the Hundred-Acre-Woods that can be used as an example.

On the Assembly Line

Objective:

To simulate an assembly line and produce a product

Teacher Preparation:

You will need a stack of white typing paper, ten scissors, five rulers, five yellow crayons, five black crayons or markers, and five pencils.

Instructions:

Tell the students that they are going to be part of an assembly line producing bookmarks. Each member of the group must follow the directions for his or her role. No one may perform the job of another person even if his or her own job is done. Students must work in the order specified in the directions.

Divide the class into groups of five. Each group works as a separate assembly line. Set up a table or a line of desks for each group's work area. Students will remain standing during production time.

The job for each worker is as follows: The first worker will use scissors to cut the typing paper into fourths. The second worker will use a ruler and pencil to draw a 4-x-3-inch rectangle on each quarter sheet. The third worker will use a yellow crayon to add a happy face to the rectangle. The fourth worker will use a black crayon or marker to put the

word "Bookmark" on each rectangle. The fifth worker will cut out the rectangle, making a stack of those finished.

If you have an uneven number of students, use the "extras" as quality control personnel. They may walk around the groups making sure that the workers are following the rules. Also, they may remove any piece of work that does not meet the high standards of the bookmark company.

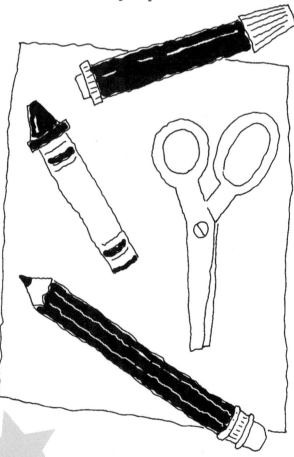

On the Assembly Line, *cont.*

Line the workers up at their stations with their materials. Set the timer for a designated amount of time. Do not go too long.

You will be surprised to see how many bookmarks can be produced in a short period of time. When the timer goes off, the groups count the number of finished products. Partial products do not count.

Be sure to take time at the end of the activity to debrief the groups. Ask the students what bothered them about the assembly line. (My job was faster/slower than the next person. The bookmarks are too sloppy. No originality was allowed in the production. The job is boring when there is no variety.) If they were to do the process again, what changes would they make? Would they prefer to work on custom jobs?

Variation:

Go through the process again, having each student complete their own set of bookmarks, doing all the jobs alone. Was the process slower? Were the finished products of higher quality? Does everyone work at the same speed? Did the number of individually made bookmarks differ from the number made by the assembly line?

Puzzling Pictures

Objective:

To examine lines and explore how parts of a picture relate spatially to each other

Teacher Preparation:

Choose two greeting cards or pictures, one very simple with little detail for primary classes, and one with more detail for intermediate classes. On the back of each picture, make a grid of thirty equal squares. Number each box of the grid from one to thirty as illustrated here. Cut both cards or pictures into the thirty equal squares, and keep the squares for each card or picture in its own envelope. Paste a copy of the uncut card or picture to the front of the envelope. Additionally, each student will need a pencil and access to crayons, markers, or colored pencils.

Instructions:

Give each student one small square of the overall picture and a piece of white typing paper or construction paper. Each child's task is to copy just the portion of the overall picture represented on his or her small square, enlarging the image to fit the typing paper. The child should attempt to make the drawing to scale, placing lines and shapes on the larger drawing where they appear on the smaller square.

Students should then color their new drawings to match their small squares.

Have students write the numbers of their small squares on the backs of their large drawings. When all of the students have completed their squares, post the finished large drawings on the wall in their numerical order. The finished product should resemble the original, uncut card or picture.

Variations:

- Enlarge or reduce the size of the paper that students draw on, depending on the wall space available to post the finished product.

- Cut the card or picture in fewer squares and allow the students to work in groups.

- Allow younger students to see the original card or picture, and be sure to make the picture simple.

The Art of Making Rubbings

Objective:

To create pictures using leaf rubbings

Teacher Preparation:

Collect a variety of leaves ahead of time or take students on a playground excursion to do so. You also will need white typing paper (tissue paper is even better) and crayons for this activity.

Instructions:

Start the lesson by having students study a favorite leaf. Talk about the shape. The edges of some leaves are smooth and others have wavy or scalloped edges. Some leaf edges have sharp points. You will even find leaves of various shapes growing on the same plant. Be sure to study the network of veins on the leaf.

A typical leaf is made up of three main parts: the *blade*, the *petiole*, and the *stipules*. The *blade* is the broad part of a leaf that holds the food-making cells. The *petiole* is the stemlike part of the leaf that holds the blade. Most *stipules* are shaped like tiny leaves and found at the base of the petiole. They add to the food-making power of the blade and help protect the leaf.

After you have studied the leaves, have the students begin their rubbings. Place the leaf on the desk, vein side up.

Cover the leaf with a piece of paper and rub with the side of a crayon. Try different sizes and shapes. Some leaves will give a better impression than others. After some practice, pass out a clean sheet of paper and start to make patterns. Encourage the students to use fall colors (green, orange, yellow, red, brown).

Variations:

- Let the students experiment with other objects (coins, paper clips, etc.). It would be fun to make a rubbings collage.

- If you have an iron available, try a leaf transfer. Rub one side of the leaf with crayon. Cover the entire surface. Place the leaf crayon-side down on paper. Cover with a second sheet. Press with the hot iron. The hot wax makes an image of the leaf on the paper. Be sure an adult supervises the use of the iron. Keep moving the iron when in contact with the paper.

Me and Myself

Objective:

To have the students create copies of themselves to fill their vacant seats when they go home for the day (This can be a fun surprise for the regular teacher when he or she returns to the classroom.)

Teacher Preparation:

Before class, bring a large rack holding butcher paper into your room. (Most elementary schools make butcher paper available this way.) Make sure one of the bolts contains white paper. Students also will need scissors, pencils, and coloring supplies.

Instructions:

This particular art project can work several different ways. Students can trace their full bodies or just from the waist up. If you have a big block of time, you can have students cut out their shapes twice, for both front and back. Staple the two sides together, leaving a space so the shapes can be stuffed with newspapers. (Obviously, this last version takes more time and would be best for older students.)

To begin the lesson, pair off the students. Together they should tear or cut paper from the rack large enough to trace two bodies or half bodies. (While the rest of the class reads silently or does a desk activity, you can assist the pairs with the paper, continuing to call two at a time until all the class has paper.)

Me and Myself, *cont.*

Have each partner trace his or her buddy and then have the two reverse roles. Be sure arms are stretched out from the body and fingers are spread apart. Together the partners cut out and color the outlines to match hair coloring and clothing. If time allows, students can color both the fronts and the backs of their figures.

Before the students go home for the day, use masking tape to attach the half or full figures to the desk chairs. The regular teacher will be greeted with a host of smiling faces when he or she returns to the classroom.

Variations:

- Have each student cut out a pocket and glue it to the chest of the cutout. During writing time, ask everyone to prepare a short note, poem, or picture for the teacher. Slip these "surprises" into the pockets when the figures are attached to the chairs.

- If you happen to be substituting around a "Curriculum Night," have the students write the notes to their parents instead of to the teacher.

Crayon Lifting

Objective:

To have fun creating a double image using chalk and crayons

Teacher Preparation:

You will need one sheet of white construction paper (cut in half) for each student. Provide two small paper clips, crayons, and a piece of chalk, either white or yellow, for each student. It is a good idea to put scratch paper or newspaper under the construction paper to keep the desk clean.

Instructions:

Have students fully chalk one-half of their construction paper, the heavier the better. Once the half-sheet is chalked, have the students color with crayons directly over the chalk on the same paper. Large blocks, curved lines, or random geometric designs are fine. (Remember, this sheet is not the actual picture. That comes next.) Encourage the students to fill this sheet with plenty of color, the bolder the better! Every space should be colored from corner to corner using lots of different crayons.

Now have the students lay the plain sheet on top of the chalked half-sheet. Paper clip the two sheets together to keep them from moving. Using a pencil, have students draw a picture, pressing hard so that the color will lift from

the chalk and imprint the back of the pencil drawing. A nature or outdoor scene works well, but leave that decision to the artists.

When they have finished, have students remove the paper clips. A colored picture will appear on the back of the pencil drawing. It is fun to mount both the picture and its reversed duplicate on a piece of colored construction paper.

Variation:

This is a good art project for introducing primary colors (red, yellow, blue) and secondary colors (orange, violet, green). Have the students choose to work with either the primary or secondary colors.

Three-Dimensional Cards

Objective:

To create note cards using a three-dimensional object as the center or focal point of the design

Teacher Preparation:

You will need small natural objects and a sheet of white construction paper for each student as well as glue, scratch paper, pencils, and coloring materials.

Instructions:

During the recess before the art period, have students collect some small natural objects (flat sticks, broad blades of grass, small flowers or petals, small leaves, etc.) to use on their note cards. Remind the class that the objects must be light enough to be glued to the paper. (Items such as rocks or pine cones will not hold.)

Drafting on scratch paper, have students create designs to put on a card. Although they can use crayons, markers, and colored pencils, they need to include one or more of the natural objects in their designs. When they are ready, have students fold their white construction paper in half twice; once horizontally, then vertically. This will form their cards. On the front cover they should draw their designs, carefully gluing the natural objects into the picture.

Allow students to choose to write a note to their teacher or to save the card for a friend or family member.

Variation:

If an indoor recess is called or the students cannot get outside to collect natural objects, design the card with a different twist. Have each student pick a geometric shape (circle, square, triangle, etc.) and create a design around that shape. They should draw their shapes on the cards with black marker or crayon to be easily visible. Then they can color around their shapes with the other colors. Encourage the students to incorporate their geometric shapes into their designs by making them, for example, the head of a dog, the center of a flower, or the window of a house.

Holey Pictures

Objective:

To create pictures made visible as light streams through them

Teacher Preparation:

Have available a variety of colored construction paper cut in half. Each student will need a straight pin and some newspaper to protect desks from scratching. Have them use white typing paper and pencils for preliminary sketching. Lay out a small box of paper clips for the class to use. Make a sample picture to show the class.

Instructions:

Students should outline a picture on a piece of white typing paper without concern for small details. When students complete their first drawings, they can choose a piece of construction paper and clip their drawings on top of it. Then, with a straight pin, they should pierce around the drawing, outlining their picture with numerous pinholes. The holes should be as close together as possible without ripping the paper. Be sure they push hard enough for the pin to go through both sheets of paper. Once they have completed the work, they should remove the white paper. Hang these "holey pictures" in the window where the light can stream through the holes to display the pictures.

Variation:

If it happens to be close to a special day (Thanksgiving, Christmas, Hanukkah, Valentine's Day, etc.), have the students design seasonal pictures and choose construction paper colors that go with the theme (orange and black, red and green, or red and pink).

No Scissors Please

Objective:

To design, tear, and glue together a picture without using scissors

Teacher Preparation:

Use construction paper scraps from the art drawer, or if no scraps are available, cut sheets of variously colored construction paper into pieces. Each student will need some of these pieces, a pencil, and a sheet of white construction paper. Have glue available for those students who do not have their own.

Instructions:

The idea of this art project is to tear shapes to create pictures instead of cutting them out. The students need to plan their pictures on scratch paper and decide what colors to use. For example, to make a snowman, the artist might tear out white circles for the body and head, add little black eyes, tear a red scarf and mittens, and shape a little hat. For the background, he or she could tear some ragged trees and place them around the snowman. This is a fun project for students because the ragged edges add distinction to the picture. Many students who cannot draw will better succeed when tearing the pieces.

When they've torn the pieces, arrange them in place on the white construction paper before starting to glue. Additional details can be added if the picture does not look complete.

Variation:

Put out buttons, felt, material, cotton balls, and other items and let students choose one to add to their pictures (felt mittens, cotton ball tail, or button nose) to lend a three-dimensional look.

Music and Physical Education

Most schools have specialists who teach music and physical education. However, if you substitute in a classroom where you are expected to teach your own classes, we have included five days worth of ideas to get you started. These suggestions can be used in both primary and intermediate grades.

Music

- Bring a mood music tape to class. Pass out drawing paper and crayons. After students listen to the music for a few minutes with eyes closed, have them draw how they feel. Pictures may be actual scenes or just lines and curves. Ask volunteers to share their "music expressions."

- Have an old-fashioned song fest. Start by teaching the class a favorite tune (make it lively or funny) and ask the students to join in on the chorus. Then invite students to request favorite songs. Some students will be willing to lead songs themselves. Invite kids to share camp songs or ones they sing at home.

- Invest in a record or cassette that has both the "Bunny Hop" and the "Hokey Pokey" on it. Most kids are familiar with both songs and love to get the chance to dance. If you are able, you can lead these dances without the record or cassette, if necessary, or check out a copy from your local or school library.

- Divide the class into two teams. Each team takes turns, singing one verse from a song they have learned during the year, or past years. Continue taking turns until one team cannot think of a new song to sing.

- Purchase a sing-along video at a video store. The videos have the words to popular songs right on the screen, with a bouncing ball to indicate wording!

Physical Education

- Divide the students into small groups and challenge them to find ways to cross the room without walking. No group can repeat an action already demonstrated by another group. Some examples might be skipping, somersaulting, hopping, scooting, twirling, and so on. After every group has had a chance to perform, make the rules harder: tell group members to hold hands and find a new way to cross the floor.

- Run some relay races. Form two or three circles. Give each group a book that can be dropped on the floor without damage (such as a phone book). Appoint a captain for each circle. The captain starts the race, balancing the book on his or her head and running around the outside of the circle. When the captain gets back to his or her own place, the person on the right races with the book. When players drop the book, they must go back to their starting places and go again. When everyone in the circle has had a turn, the book should be back in the hands of the captain who then tells the group to sit. The first group sitting down is the winner. Hands cannot

be used except to place the book on the head. Younger students can try balancing a small book on one up-turned palm without using the other hand.

- Form equal lines with six to eight students in each. If the lines are not even, some students may have to take two turns. Give the first person in each line a three-foot length of rope or piece of heavy string tied in a circle. The first person must pass the rope or string over his or her head and body, step out of it, and pass it on to the next person. Once the whole group has taken a turn, they should sit to show that they are finished.

- Try the good, old game Simon Says. Use the instructions to give the class a good workout (jumping jacks, hopping, etc.). Invite a student to be the next Simon.

- If the school has a track, take the students outside and see how many laps they can run. Have a time-out spot identified so they will know where to go if they get winded. Encourage walking if jogging is too difficult.

PART III

Are You Ready for Anything?

How Would You Handle These Situations?

How Would You Handle These Situations? Quiz

Directions: Circle the responses that you feel would best solve the following problems. Recommended responses are given following the exercise.

1. Coming back from morning recess, two students are pushing and shoving each other. Would you

   a. ignore the situation?

   b. remind the students of correct manners?

   c. write a reprimand for the home-room teacher to see?

   d. have students go to a time-out center in the classroom and work out their differences?

2. Things have gotten a bit noisy in the classroom. You are having a hard time settling the students down. Just then the principal walks into your room. Would you

   a. raise your voice and ask students to be quiet?

   b. walk to the board and conspicuously place a chalk X mark on it?

   c. sit down at the teacher's desk and start to read silently?

   d. apologize to the principal for the disorderly conduct of the class?

3. In the middle of math class a student approaches you and says she is going to be sick. Would you

   a. tell her to run to the bathroom?

   b. ask her to move to the sink?

   c. find a wastebasket or paper bag for her to use?

   d. remind her to stand in one spot and not move around?

4. You are doing an art project and you notice one of the students is getting frustrated. He throws down the activity and refuses to work on it. Would you

   a. demand that he finish the activity?

   b. ask another student who seems to be doing well to assist him and work as a partner?

   c. keep him in at recess to complete the project?

   d. tell him that he is excused from the activity?

5. You have just dismissed the class when you notice handouts from the office that were supposed to go home that day. You forgot to pass them out. Would you

    a. toss the handouts in the wastebasket?

    b. return them to the office?

    c. send them home the next day?

    d. grab a few students who are still standing around the door, give them each a few copies, and ask them to find as many classmates as the can?

6. You have an errand to run at lunch time and you are afraid you will not get back on time. Would you

    a. tell the teacher next door that you might be late and ask her to watch out for your students?

    b. notify the office secretary so he or she can have someone cover for you if you do not get back on time?

    c. hurry and go so you can get back on time?

    d. skip the errand and do it after school or on another day?

7. You have not had time to check the fire-drill routine and an unexpected drill is called. Would you

    a. grab the grade book or class list so you can do a roll call once you are outside?

    b. find the nearest outside door and exit through it?

    c. have the first student in line hold the door for the whole class?

    d. walk the class to the field or an area away from the building?

Now check your answers with the Recommended Responses given on pages 82 and 83. Give yourself one point for each correct letter circled.

Recommended Responses

1. b. is a good response for a temporary solution. However, if the problem continues, try **d.** Sometimes it is a good idea to let the offending students work out a solution together. (Directions for setting up a time-out area are included in this book under Practical Ideas for Classroom Management and Motivation, p. 12.)

2. Both **b.** and **c.** Briskly put a chalk X mark on the board and then sit at your desk and pick up a book. The students will quickly notice that you are ignoring their behavior. Some students will immediately sit down and then they will start monitoring their peers. If the noise does not subside, add a second chalk mark to the first. Raising your voice will only add to the noise in the room. The principal will be pleased that you can control the class without his or her intervention. You decide whether you want to attach a consequence to the chalk marks. Usually the mark is enough in itself.

3. Both **c.** and **d.** You are doing the custodian a big favor if you reject a. and b. Using the sink can clog the drain, and no none wants to follow a sick student with a mop to the bathroom, often leaving puddles along the way. Have them stand in one spot and use a paper bag or wastebasket if available.

4. b. Students may listen to a classmate even when they are not willing to let a teacher help. Be careful about excusing a student from an activity. Other pupils may ask for the same exemption. The trick here is to try to assist the student before frustration sets in.

5. c., if the notice was not about a meeting to be held that night. However, if the material is dated, you might try **d.** At least some of the students will receive the message. Many of them have brothers and sisters in the school who will be carrying the same handout so all is not lost. After all, you're just human and doing the best job you can.

6. d. is the only answer. When you are substituting in a classroom, do not count on others to do your job. The errand will have to wait.

7. a., b., c., d. If you answered yes to all four choices, you are on the right track. The main concern is getting the students out of the building in a safe and orderly manner. Once you reach your destination, you should do a quick roll call to make sure all the class is with you. We hope this situation serves as a reminder that you should always check fire-drill protocol as soon as possible after you enter a school.

What do your scores mean?

0-1 correct: Reread Part I for practical ideas to increase your classroom comfort.

2-3 correct: Check out the classroom management section again for more ideas.

4-5 correct: You're on your way! With a well-stocked Sub Kit and a sense of humor, your proficiency will continue to increase.

6-7 correct: Super Sub! You are ready to tackle any classroom!

Have a Few Free Minutes?

Each of the following ideas provides a guided activity when you have a few extra minutes. Many of these activities can be done as a class by making a transparency for the overhead projector, or individually by handing out copies of the activity sheet to each student.

- Play "Tell Me When..."

  Have students stand in front of the class. Give them one of the following story starters and ask them to spontaneously tell a story based on it. You can give them a one minute time limit, or allow them to complete their story.

Variations:

- Have students write their story instead of telling it aloud. Ask for volunteers to read their stories.

- Present a "tag-team" story where one student begins the story and then tags another student to continue speaking after thirty seconds. Students continue to tag other students at thirty-second intervals, until the story is completed.

- Have students write the story starters for each other.

"Tell Me When..." Story Starter Ideas

- you became a hero."
- you got locked in a chocolate factory."
- you broke a world's record."
- you were captured by pirates."
- you fell out of an airplane."
- you found a dollar in your hamburger."

School Word Find

Find all the listed words in the word find below:

Word List:

apple	desk	pencil	students
bell	education	read	study
book	eraser	recess	teach
backpack	library	ruler	write
chalk	lunch	scissors	youngsters
classroom	math	stickers	

```
H A V M W T S S E K Y U I S
F T Y X A B C R D A E R P T
D G M B W T V O U D R O K U
S E A A O L U S C H A L K D
R J S C E O W S A Q S I L E
E I O K B R K I T E E B H N
T A P P L E U C I D R R U T
S R M A D C L S O H T A M S
G S N C M E J L N F L R T W
N Z C K M S T U D Y I Y R H
U A C L A S S R O O M P E C
O P E N C I L N O H A S L N
Y W R I T E A C H P T R U U
B S R E K C I T S G M L R L
```

Make transparencies for each of the six puzzles below. Project one of the puzzles and have students find as many words as they can, going ANY direction. The minimum length of words depends on the age of the students.

Word Creation

Find as many words as you can in the puzzles.

Puzzle 1:
```
C  A  N  D
B  E  A  F
L  S  P  N
R  E  I  G
```

Puzzle 2:
```
E  D  A  V
G  S  L  E
A  T  N  M
R  U  Y  M
```

Puzzle 3:
```
R  O  S  A
O  U  G  P
A  A  N  L
O  V  L  E
```

Puzzle 4:
```
O  W  E  N
K  G  H  E
P  E  A  T
J  H  R  D
```

Puzzle 5:
```
O  V  R  T
R  U  Y  P
A  G  E  J
T  F  L  O
```

Puzzle 6:
```
R  T  N  W
E  W  T  C
V  A  I  J
A  H  D  L
```

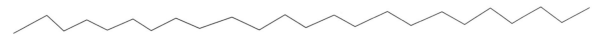

Mystery Cross-Words

Use the word list provided to correctly fill in the grid. (This puzzle
is like a crossword puzzle, except there are no clues.)

Four Letters	Five Letters	Six Letters	Seven Letters	Eight Letters
read	spell	rulers	history	alphabet
math	lunch	eraser	science	
book	study	spiral		
work	paper	binder		
word	rules			
edit				

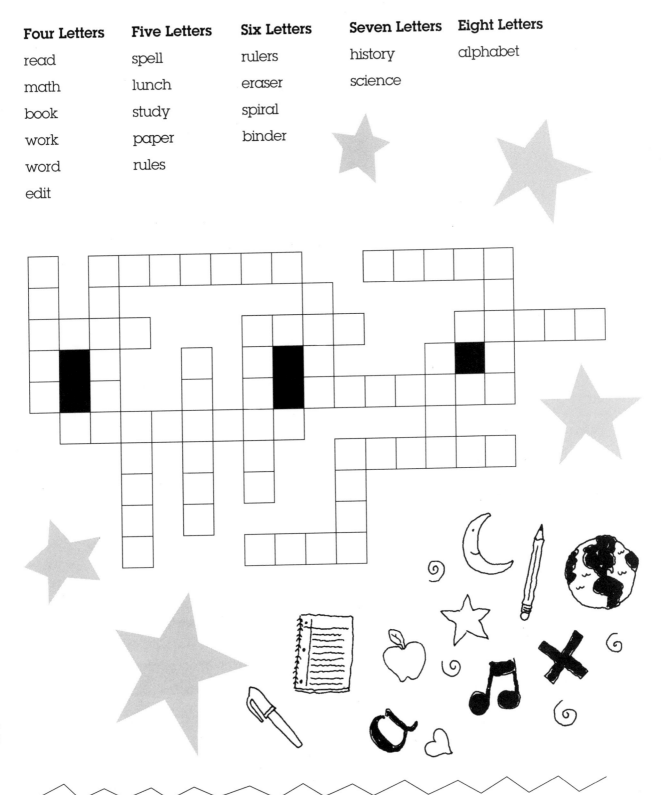

What Are We Learning?

Directions: Complete the crossword puzzle using the clues provided.

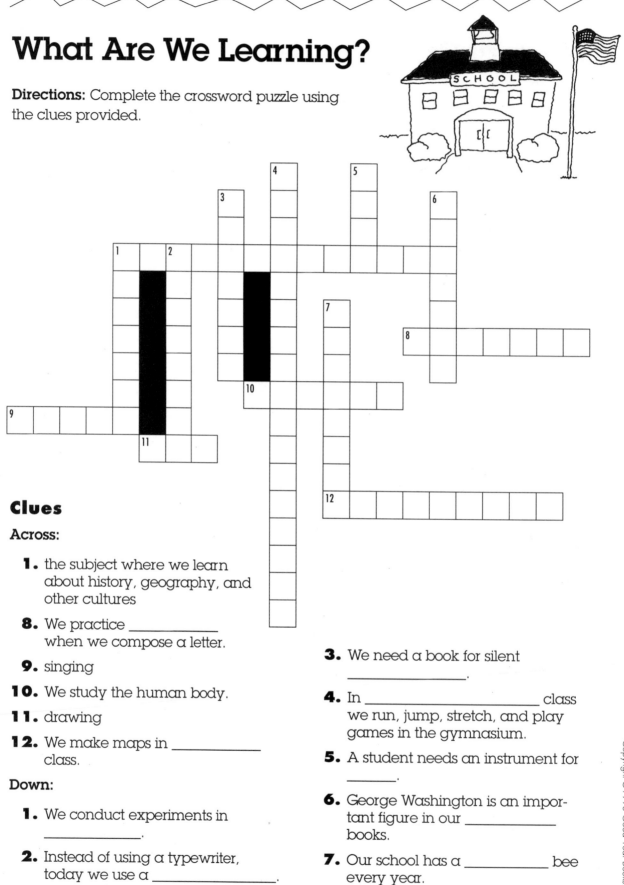

Clues

Across:

1. the subject where we learn about history, geography, and other cultures

8. We practice _____ when we compose a letter.

9. singing

10. We study the human body.

11. drawing

12. We make maps in _____ class.

Down:

1. We conduct experiments in _____.

2. Instead of using a typewriter, today we use a _____.

3. We need a book for silent _____.

4. In _____ class we run, jump, stretch, and play games in the gymnasium.

5. A student needs an instrument for _____.

6. George Washington is an important figure in our _____ books.

7. Our school has a _____ bee every year.

Answers

School Word Find

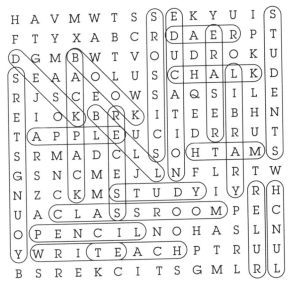

What Are We Learning?

Across:
1. Social Studies
8. Writing
9. Music
10. Health
11. Art
12. Geography

Down:
1. Science
2. Computer
3. Reading
4. Physical Education
5. Band
6. History
7. Spelling
9. Math

Mystery Cross-Words

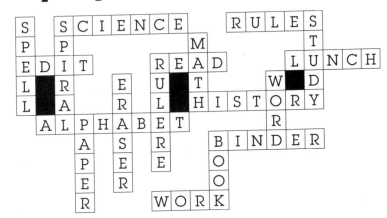

Spelling Puzzle Grid

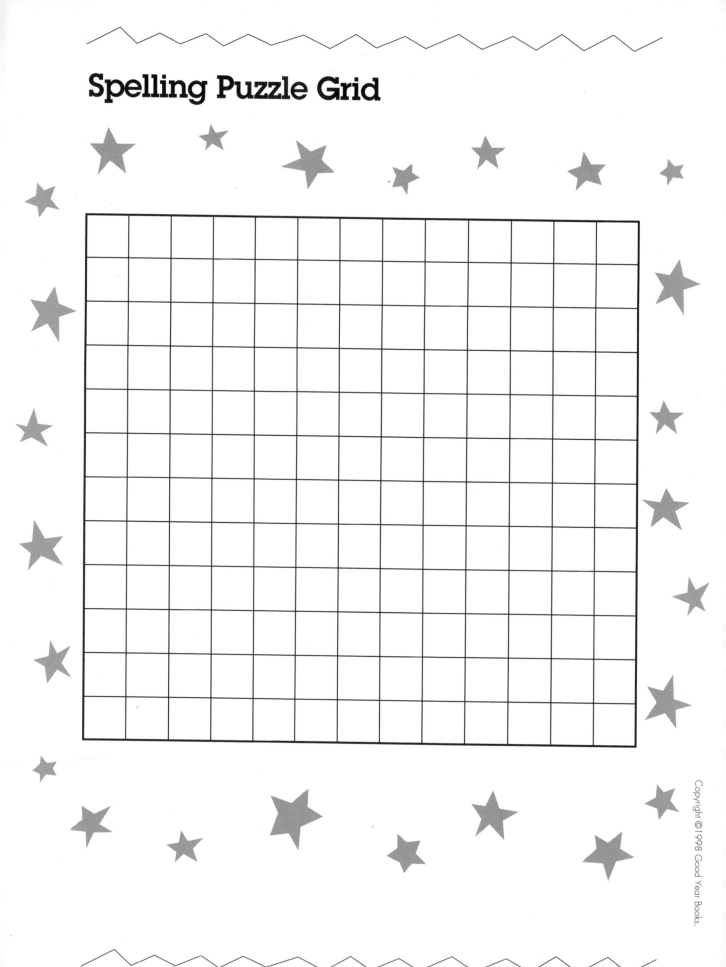

About the Authors

Cary Seeman, who is now retired, taught elementary school for 23 years. She has a B.A. in journalism and an M.A. in administration. She lives half of the year in Renton, Washington, and half of the year in Apache Junction, Arizona.

Shannon Hofstrand, daughter of coauthor Cary Seeman, is a junior high English and drama instructor. She has a B.A. in English and an M.A. in school counseling. She lives in Bonney Lake, Washington, with her daughter, Eryn.